Day One: Now What?

Deena Casagrande

Day One: Now What?
2016 by Deena Casagrande

Printed in the United States of America

Cover Design by CreateSpace (Love this team!)

Illustrations by Deena Casagrande
Church illustration courtesy of Google images
(ons8.dromikh.top)

Casagrande, Deena M
West Chester Ohio

Day One: Now What?

1. Religion. 2. Spirituality

ISBN 978-0-9975933-0-3 for print version

ISBN 978-0-9975933-1-0 for Kindle e-book version

Dedication:

I would like to dedicate this book to God, who made it possible for me to be the messenger. He gave me the ideas, skills, and resources. Without Him, we have nothing.

I would like to dedicate this book to all of the people who have walked out their faith and brought someone into the Kingdom. God's grace and love is a beautiful gift to be shared with everyone.

A special dedication goes to my children, James and Rachel. I hope you feel God's love and grace every day of your journey!

Congratulations!

You have made a decision to accept Jesus Christ as your Lord and Savior[a]. You have confessed your sins and have been forgiven. You are now an adopted child of God and heir to His Kingdom[b]!

Before you became a Christian, you likely wondered what would happen to you after you die. Now you know! You will go to live in an eternal heaven free from sin, pain, and sickness. You are free because Jesus paid the price for all of your sins—but what does all this mean here in this life?

---

[a] John 3:16
[b] Galatians 4:7

You were born with a God-shaped hole in your heart. God has spent your entire life calling you by name[c], asking you to join Him, and showing you Himself through His creation[d]. You may not have noticed or maybe did not believe that a special person in your life or a miracle was from God. You may have spent your life trying to fill that empty, God-shaped hole with something else—people, career, sports, food, drink, drugs, sex—but nothing ever satisfied or took away that longing desire. Just like a key in a lock, God fits into that God-shaped hole perfectly[e]. You are on your way to living a life of contentment and fulfillment, but how?

---

[c] John 10:3
[d] 2 Corinthians 5:17
[e] John 6:35

There is a secret that the world does not want you to know: You can be happy. You can have hope. You can have peace. It is not through what you have or what you do. It is through who you are—a new creation in Christ.

If you are asked who you are, do you answer with your name and job title or favorite hobby? Your identity is in things that will end. You will get a new job or retire. You will get a new hobby or lose the ability one day to enjoy your current hobby. If your identity is in *who* you are as a person—a child of God, a prince or princess, an heir to His Kingdom, beloved member of His family forever—you will find new meaning to the life you have been living.

Today, as a new Christian, you may or may not feel different. Today you may feel like your eyes have been opened and the world looks brighter, or it may still look dingy and dirty. Do not lose hope. There is a way to unlock the riches in your inheritance; these are things far beyond gold and silver, stock options, or toys. Life is a journey, and your decision has led you to walk a new path toward a better future.

This book summarizes the main points you need to start this new walk—like points on a roadmap. Read this today and maybe several times in the next month to help you continue along the path you have chosen. You may be feeling very excited about the journey or a little uneasy about the road ahead. It will be well worth it!

Life in this world without Christ is like playing a game of football. Everyone is tackling everyone else to get the elusive (materialistic) ball home in order to score points (success). Players come and go, but the ball is the focus of the game. Today, instead of shoulder pads and a helmet, you woke up in a baseball uniform. Look out! You are playing a new game with a new set of rules.

Life in this world with Christ is like playing a game of baseball. The ball is hit away to move the player around the field to home in order to score. The ball is only a tool. The player is the focus of the game.

If you have been playing football all your life and suddenly decide to play baseball, you must learn the rules and practice the skills needed to play. You are not born with the ability to play baseball but you may be gifted in some skills.

Just as in baseball, your new life in Christ will take some practice. You may feel alive for the first time and want to experience more. Help from "coaches" can show you the skills to keep this new, fresh feeling. Christian believers that you know or are going to meet—a church pastor, church members, small group members, family members, or mentors—can be good coaches. Make sure they have mastered the skills you are looking to learn from them. Practice of the new skills will help you adjust to the new "game of life."

Finding a Church

The first thing to do is find a church where you can get involved[f]. You can go to a church where a family member or friend attends or try a church nearby. If you're unsure where to start, ask the person or organization that helped you take your first step in your walk with Christ. Find out what the church believes, meet the pastor, and attend a Bible study group to get to know people. Don't just go to the Sunday morning service. Volunteering is an excellent way to get involved. Churches often have special projects in the community and there is always work to be done to make the church run. You will meet

---

[f] 1 Corinthians 12:12-13

others who believe in Jesus and can encourage

you while you learn valuable skills.

Reading the Bible

The next thing you need is a Bible; this is the guidebook God has given us to help us on our journey with Him[g]. Some translations are easier to read than others. *The Message* and *New Living Translation* Bibles use common English. There are also some good study Bibles that have helpful explanations of the text. Bibles can be found at bookstores, grocery stores, department stores, or online. Some churches give away Bibles or New Testaments (the second half of the full Christian Bible).

Once you've found a translation you like, start reading the New Testament. Matthew is the first New Testament book and is found in the

[g] Mark 13:31

middle of the Bible. This will take you through the life of Jesus and the start of the church all the way to the last book of Revelation. You can then go back and read the Old Testament starting in Genesis for the history of man[h]. Reading and studying the Bible will help you understand God, the church, and His plan and blessings for us[i].

(The Bible verses listed at the bottom of the pages in this book are for readers to look up for further study.)

---

[h] Luke 1:1-2
[i] Luke 11:28

Praying with Purpose

The next skill to practice is prayer. It can seem intimidating, especially to a brand new Christian, yet prayer is simply talking to God. The best way to grow this new skill is to pray with a purpose. As a new Christian, the feelings of forgiveness and freedom may be difficult to comprehend. Prayer will help strengthen these feelings. To pray with a purpose, pray daily for the following five things:

1. *Confess your sins to God.*

2. *Ask for forgiveness.*

3. *Forgive others and yourself.*

4. *Ask for direction from God.*

5. *Surrender.*

1.   Confess your sins to God.

Confession is admitting the things you have done wrong. Be specific about the sins and tell them to God. Ask Him to help you stop doing those things. With God's help and praying daily, the wrong choices will become more obvious[j]. No person is perfect, but it can get easier to do the right thing with practice.

If you feel that your sins are too great or too many to be forgiven, please do not lose hope. Jesus died for all of your sins[k], not just the ones of your past. He gives us the Holy Spirit to give us power over sin[l] and the Word to help us correct our behavior.

---

[j] 1 John 1:9
[k] Colossians 2:13
[l] Romans 15:13

2.   Ask God for forgiveness of the confessed sins.

Believing that God forgives you for every sin can be overwhelming. It is written in the Bible that all of our sins are recorded in the books to be read at our judgment[m]. If we have accepted Jesus as our Lord and Savior, He will step forward and show God that all of the sins were wiped clean from the books, because He paid the price[n]. Asking forgiveness daily will help you feel forgiven, and practice will strengthen your faith in God and your relationship with Him.

---

[m] Revelation 20:12
[n] Romans 8:33-34

3.   Forgive others and yourself.

Most of us have a mental list of people that have done things to hurt us. Make a list of the names and read this list to God daily. Even if the pain of the betrayal still hurts, forgiving them is an act of love for your heart—not them. Day-by-day, the act of forgiving will help heal your heart and will give you peace[o].

Forgiving yourself for the things you have done may be the hardest thing to do. This may take daily practice before you begin to accept that God has forgiven you. The enemy may tell you lies such as, "You are not worthy," or "You are too bad to be forgiven." The truth is that no one is worthy to be forgiven; we are all sinners,

---

[o] Mark 11:25

but God forgives us anyway[p]. That is His grace. You may find this grace in others who have forgiven you for horrible things you have done to them. You must seek God's grace for yourself and others. Look in the mirror, tell yourself, "I forgive you for (insert sin here), you are more than your sin, you are a child of God and He chose to forgive you." By practicing daily, you will find the grace and peace that can only come from God.

---

[p] Romans 3:23

4. *Ask for direction from God.*

It is written in the Bible that God has a plan for each of us even before we are born[q]. If you are not sure of what it means to be a Christian, this prayer will help you. Ask God to show you His plan for you[r]. Ask Him to open doors and put people in your life to help you. You will see amazing things happen just because you asked. Non-believers may look at them as coincidences, but you will know these are God's answers to you.

---

[q] Jeremiah 1:5
[r] Jeremiah 29:11

5.   *Surrender.*

This can be the hardest prayer for a new Christian. Make a list of everything that you struggle with in your life. Read that list to God and ask Him to help you fix those things. Addictions, harmful behavior, bad habits, and misplaced priorities can leave a person in misery. God wants to deliver everyone from these "prisons." Give them to God daily[s]. Ask for help from fellow Christians[t]. Christian counselors can help with the large problems such as addictions and behaviors. Ask for prayer from others. Turn in a prayer request to church (each church has its own method of receiving prayer requests for a team to pray over).

---

[s] Psalm 55:22
[t] 1 Peter 5:5

God wants to be a part of our lives. Prayer is our way of talking with God. As we grow in relationship with Him we can find ways to include Him in our everyday lives and speak with a closeness—a familiarity. There may be days when we do not have the words and just need to listen. With each day, prayer will get easier and easier[u].

---

[u] Romans 12:12

Good skills become a habit after being practiced for anywhere from 18 days to 6 months[v]. For every bad habit you give up, you must replace it with a good habit. Attending church, reading the Bible, and praying with purpose are habits that will build a foundation for your new life in Christ. If you practice them you will see other skills become habits, such as being kind to others, speaking the truth, and helping people in need. When you are busy practicing your new skills, you will find you do not have the time or energy to get into trouble. There are good deeds waiting to be done everywhere. Your opportunities await. With

---

[v] Lally, Phillippa. *European Journal of Social Psychology*

these small steps you will see good things happen

and enjoy life as you have never seen it before.

There is one word of caution: The enemy, Satan, is an angel that fell from heaven after challenging God. He and his army of demons look for ways to interrupt our relationships with God and others[w]. Do not lose hope or faith when times are tough. Christians struggle with life, too—but they have great options for help and escape. Ask for help!

You have lived your life until today playing football, chasing after the empty things this world has to offer. With the help of your new coaches and skills you are ready to play baseball. As you round the bases for home, you will experience good days and bad—but you have Jesus to help you navigate them. Best of all, remember that the

---

[w] 1 Peter 5:8

journey will end in heaven for an eternity of love, joy, and peace[x].

God Bless You!

---

[x] Philippians 4:6-7

Bibliography

The Bible. Print. King James Version.

The Holy Bible, New Living Translation is a registered trademark of Tyndale House Publishing.

Lally, Phillipa, et al. "How are habits formed: Modelling habit formation in the real world." *European Journal of Social Psychology*. 40, (2010): 998-1009. Web. 16 July, 2009. Wiley Online Library.

The Message is a registered trademark of NavPress Publishing Co.